Level _
Pre-Reader

Book 1: Letter sounds r, a, m

Amanda Riccetti
Illustrations by Steven Gomez

Library of Congress Control Number: 2019911840
Published in the United States by Kindle Direct Publishing, an Amazon Company, Seattle, WA.
www.kdp.amazon.com
www.readingwithmissamanda.com

Library of Congress Cataloging-in-Publication Data

Riccetti, Amanda, 2019 –
Reading with Miss Amanda, Level 1: Pre-Reader—Book 1: Focusing on learning the letter sounds r, a, m
by Amanda Riccetti; Illustrations by Steven Gomez, Design by Robert Riccetti
p. cm.
Summary: In the Level 1 Yellow series, Miss Amanda uses phonetic learning to teach 15 letters using the Montessori three-part lesson.
ISBN-13: 978-1-950675-65-4 | ISBN-10: 1-950675-65-3

Printed in the United States of America

This book is dedicated to every child who wants to learn how to read and the adult in their life who wants to support them.

Contents

What to Expect

PHONETIC LEARNING: Throughout this series, children learn letter sound recognition. In the Montessori Method, we do not call letters "ABC" but rather refer to their sound. Use the phonetic letter sounds listed below to become familiar with the way the sounds will be written throughout the books. Remember to always call letters by their sounds.

PHONETIC LETTER SOUNDS: a- ah, b- buh, c- ck, d- duh, e- eh, f- Fff, g- guh, h- Hhh, i- ih, j- juh, k- ck, l- Lll, m- Mmm, n- Nnn, o- oh, p- /p/, q- kwa, r- Rrr, s- Sss, t- /t/, u- uh, v- Vvv, w- wuh, x- ks, y- yuh, z- Zzz

INTUITIVE LESSONS: The lessons in the *Reading with Miss Amanda* series will feel completely intuitive to children, even if they have different styles of learning. The illustrations and games help to engage younger children at the beginning, then evolve into appealing exercises that will teach your child to read.

TIME SPENT: Expect to spend about 10-20 minutes per day on the book for five days a week. Each book could take as little as one week to master or up to two months, depending on the pace of the child and the level the child is on.

REPETITION IS GOOD: Children love repetition, and it drives learning. For example, the popular book *Goodnight Moon* by Margaret Wise Brown might bore an adult, but children love the repetition of phrases. So if you use this book and think, "that's repetitive," remember — it is designed that way.

Reading with Miss Amanda

5 levels

Level	Typical Age*	Reading Level**	Example
L1	3+ Pre-Reader	Has not learned letter sounds yet	"ah," "buh," "ck"
L2	4+ Becoming a Reader	Has not learned to phonetically read three-letter words yet	"Max," "rat," "cat"
L3	4+ Beginning Reader	Has not learned to read short sentences yet	"The crab ran and hid."
L4	4+ Budding Reader	Has not learned to read four or five-letter words in short sentences yet	"The crab ran on the sand."
L5	5+ Advanced Reader	Has not learned silent vowels (cake) or blended vowels (oo, ai) yet	"The cook baked a cake."

*The ages listed are merely guidelines that Montessori teachers use as a basis to introduce reading lessons.

**This series is also ideal for older children who need to learn reading or children with a learning difference, such as dyslexia.

If you have any issues, go to the FAQs at the end of the book.

Hi there! My name is Miss Amanda, and I'm a Montessori teacher. Welcome to my class! In this book, you will find lessons and games that will help you learn to read.
Come join me!

m
a
cat
rat
Max
a
ai
snail

Lesson 1

Identification: Learning Three Letters

Tip

When children are introduced to something new, they very often forget how to do it. Remember to keep it fun, and stop when your child is not enjoying the lesson.

It's okay to guide your child's hand if they seem to need your help when tracing letters.

Extension Lesson

Since reading and writing go hand in hand, we need to also introduce writing the letters. A fun and easy way for young children to practice writing letters is to get a shallow pan and pour cornmeal into it. Spread a thin layer and have your child write the letter with their index and middle fingers. Shake the pan to erase the letter. Then, your child can write again. This tactile experience will help your child remember the letters. Your child will love to draw in it!

Let's learn the sounds that letters make so you can learn to read!
Let's get started!

Here is the first letter. It makes the sound "Rrr."
Can you say "Rrr" for "ram"?
Now, let's write the letter "Rrr." Trace the letter "Rrr" with two fingers, then say "Rrr" for "ram."
Do this three times for me.
r

r

Nice work!
This letter makes the sound "ah."
Can you say "ah" for "apple"?
Now, let's write the letter "ah." Trace the letter "ah" with two fingers, then say "ah" for "apple."
Do this three times for me.
a

Nice work!
This letter makes the sound "Mmm."
Can you say "Mmm" for "monkey"?
Now, let's write the letter "Mmm." Trace the letter "Mmm" with two fingers, then say "Mmm" for "monkey."
Do this three times for me.
m

Lesson 2

Identification: Identifying Letters

Tip

This lesson helps your child associate a letter with the beginning sound of a picture. Have your child repeat the sound after you read it. For example, after you say "Rrr" for "rat," have your child say "Rrr" for "rat."

Extension Lesson

Take a piece of paper and write a large letter. Then, have your child trace the letter with a #2 pencil. It's okay to guide your child's hand. Say the letter sound with your child each time they trace it. Do this for each letter.

Let's learn the sounds that letters make so you can learn to read!
Let's get started!
m
a
a

Can you say "Rrr" for "ram"?

Now, repeat after me...

“Rrr” for “rat”

“Rrr” for “robin”

“Rrr” for “robot”

“Rrr” for “rocket”

Nice work!

Can you say "ah" for "apple"?

Now, repeat after me...

“ah” for “alligator”

“ah” for “acrobat”

“ah” for “ant”

“ah” for “astronaut”

Nice work!

Can you say "Mmm" for "mouse"?

Now, repeat after me...

"Mmm" for "money"

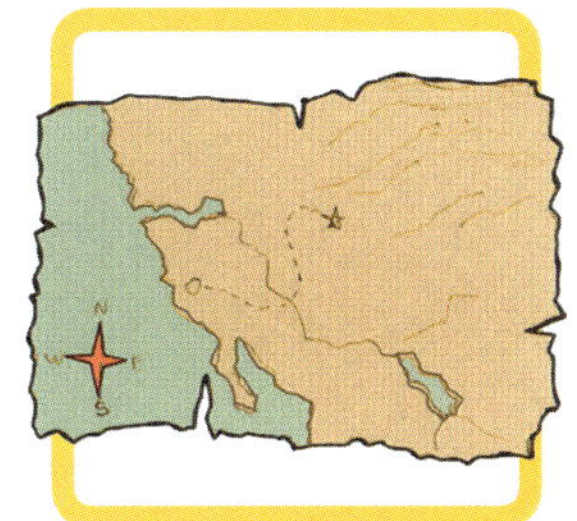

"Mmm" for "map"

"Mmm" for "mug"

"Mmm" for "moon"

Nice work!

Let's review. Practice makes permanent!

Can you trace your finger from each letter to the picture that starts with that letter?

Can you trace your finger from each picture to the letter that it sounds like?

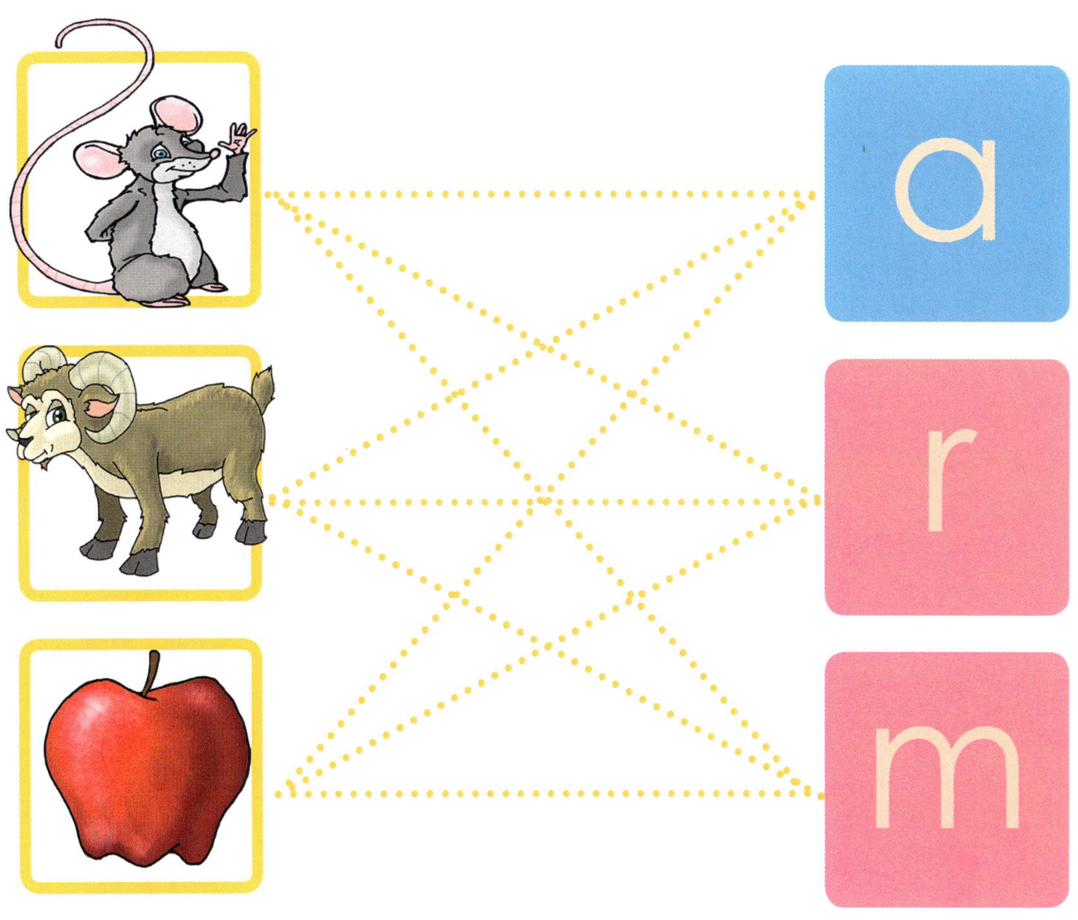

Lesson 3

Recognition Game: Guess the Letter

Tip

If your child struggles with this lesson, STOP for the day. The next day, start from Lesson 1. You will notice your child will have more confidence going through the lessons as they master the letters. Repeat this each day until they master the letters. Follow your child's pace. Remember, children love repetition, and it drives learning.

Extension Lesson

Place objects on a low table in one room. Go to another room and invite your child to play the retrieval game. Say the first letter sound of the name of one object in the first room. Ask your child to go and retrieve that object from the table. When your child retrieves all of the objects, they win the game. This game can be played in many ways. Have fun with it!

Now, let's see how many letters you remember with a game I call "Guess the Letter." Each time the page turns, the letters will change their places. Let's play!

Can you point to the letter that sounds like “Rrr” for “ram”?

Tip

If child finds "Rrr"...	You are correct!
If not...	That's okay! It's right here, it says "Rrr."

Okay, I mixed them up this time. I bet you can't find the letter "ah" for "apple."

Tip

If child finds "ah"...	You are correct!
If not...	That's okay! It's right here, it says "ah."

Last one! This time I REALLY mixed the letters up. I bet you can't find it this time! Where is the letter "Mmm" for "monkey"?

Tip

If child finds "Mmm"...	You are correct!
If not...	That's okay! It's right here, it says "Mmm."

Lesson 4

Recall Game: Abracadabra

Tip

If your child struggles with recognizing the letters, help them find the letter and stop for the day. When you return to the book, start from Lesson 1.

Extension Lesson

Find small objects, such as beads, feathers, seeds, and/or stickers whose names start with a letter that your child is learning. Cut out the letter from card stock and glue the objects on. Once the letter is created, have your child say the sound and hang it up for your child to enjoy. Make one letter for each sound your child is learning. This visual reminder will help your child recall letters.

Ready to play a game called
"Abracadabra"? Let's play!
r
a
m
a
ai
snail

Wave your hand over the first tile and say "Abracadabra."
Now, let's turn the page...

Wow, can you tell me the letter that magically appeared?

Tip

If child finds "Rrr"...	You are correct!
If not...	That's okay! It's right here, it says "Rrr."

Let’s see if you can do that again! Wave your hand over the middle tile and say “Abracadabra.”
Turn the page...

Wow, another letter appeared!
Can you tell me the letter?

Tip

If child finds "ah"...	You are correct!
If not...	That's okay! It's right here, it says "ah."

Wave your hand over the last tile and say "Abracadabra."
Turn the page...

You're good at this!
What letter is it this time?

Tip

If child finds "Mmm"...	You are correct!
If not...	That's okay! It's right here, it says "Mmm."

Lesson 5

Recall Game: Knock-Knock

Tip

If your child struggles with recognizing the letters, help them say the letter and stop for the day. When you return to the book, start from Lesson 1.

Extension Lesson

Make letters out of clay, and have your child guess the letter sounds. Your child can also make letters out of clay and have you guess them.

Welcome to
Miss Amanda's
Montessori
Classroom
Ready to use your imagination and play a game I call "Knock-Knock"? Let's see which letters are visiting today to hang out with my cat, Spunky!

Knock-knock
Who's there?

It's the letter ___!
r

Knock-knock
Who's there?

It's the letter ___!
a

Knock-knock
Who's there?

It's the letter ___!
m
Nice work!
Did you see my cat, Spunky? I wonder what he does when I'm not home!

Lesson 6

Recall Game: I Spy

Tip

Recall is the last step to make sure your child can recognize the letters. If your child struggles, you can always STOP for the day. When you return to the book, start from Lesson 1.

Extension Lesson

To help your child retain the letters they just learned, they can play a fun game I call "Fish for Sounds." To play this game, you will need string, a magnet, a short stick, card stock, a marker, and paper clips. Fasten one end of the string to the magnet and the other end to a short stick. Cut the card stock into squares two inches by two inches. With the marker, draw the letters your child is learning. Attach a paper clip to each letter card. Lay the cards face up on the floor and ask your child to "fish for the sounds"! Lay the cards face down to play "Recall" and ask your child the sound of the letter they catch.

Now, use your imagination to play a game called "I Spy." Off we go!

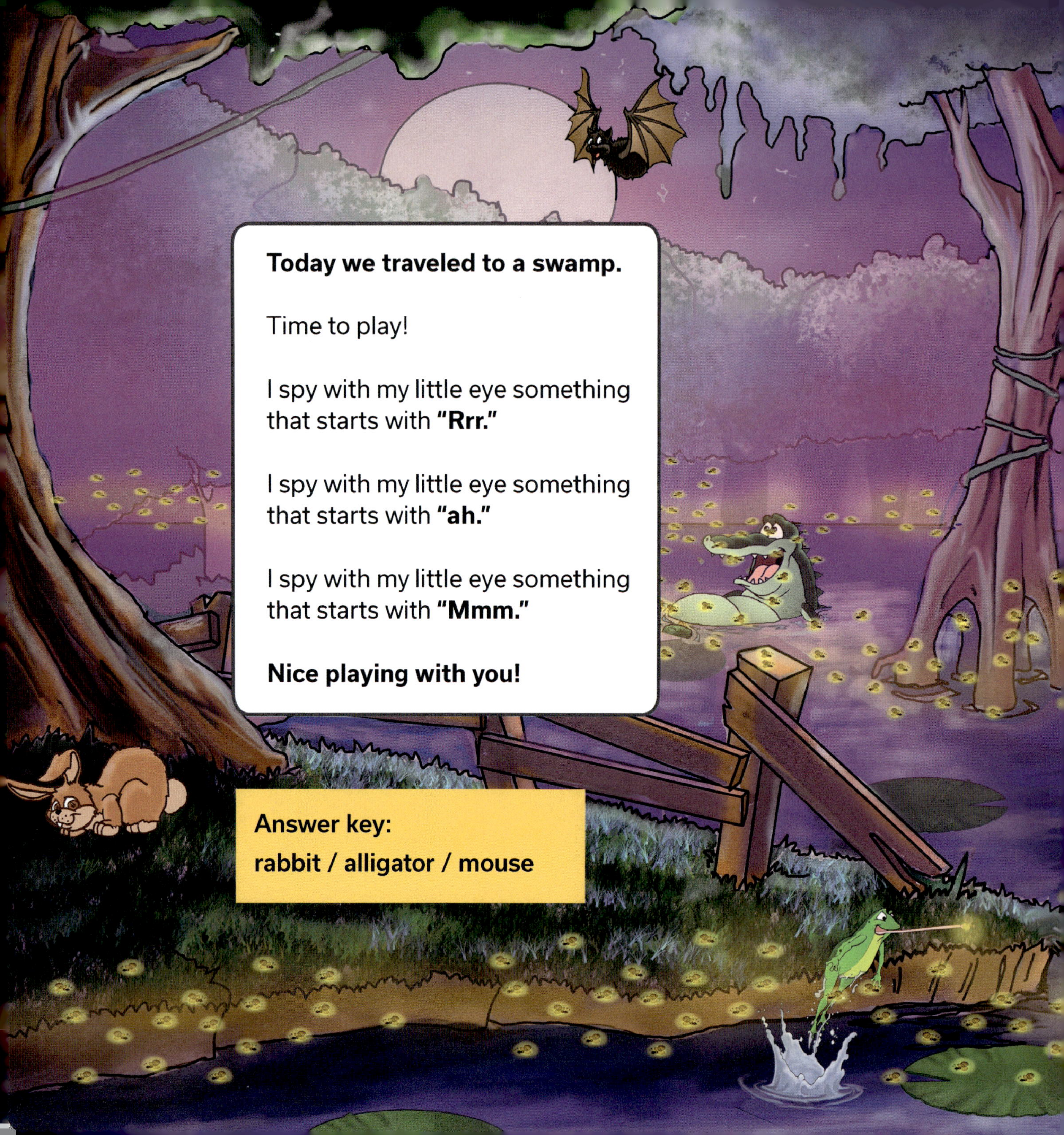

Today we traveled to a swamp.

Time to play!

I spy with my little eye something that starts with **"Rrr."**

I spy with my little eye something that starts with **"ah."**

I spy with my little eye something that starts with **"Mmm."**

Nice playing with you!

Answer key:
rabbit / alligator / mouse

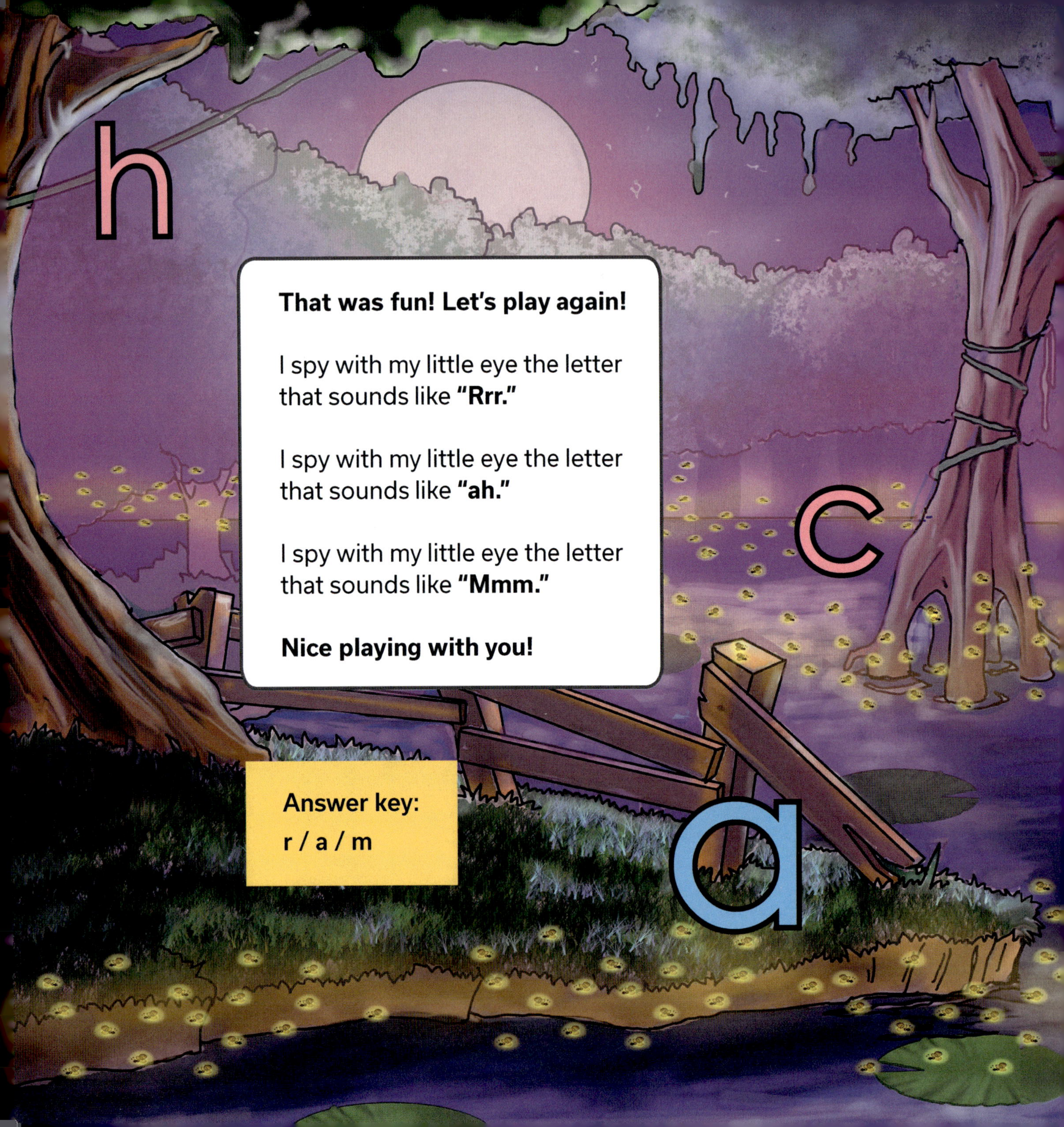

That was fun! Let's play again!

I spy with my little eye the letter that sounds like **"Rrr."**

I spy with my little eye the letter that sounds like **"ah."**

I spy with my little eye the letter that sounds like **"Mmm."**

Nice playing with you!

Answer key:
r / a / m

s
m
r

Did you know you just spelled the word **"Rrr-ah-Mmm, ram"** with the letters you are learning?
Now, for one more game...

r
a
m

Can you find eight "ah's"?

Have fun counting. See you soon!
Letter
Letter
Letter

m
a
a
cat
rat
Max
ai
DO NOT TURN THIS PAGE UNLESS YOUR CHILD HAS MASTERED THIS BOOK.

Great Job!
Congratulations!
You reached your goal. You completed Yellow Book 1. This golden ram is for you. Keep up the hard work, and I look forward to seeing you in the next book!

Accomplishments

The stamp is a symbol of your hard work. When you complete stamps for all the levels, you will be an advanced reader.

L 1

Book 1 Book 2 Book 3 Book 4 Book 5

L 2

L 3

L 4

L 5

FAQ

How much time should I spend on the book?

- Daily repetition is the best way to learn new information. If you skip days, you may end up repeating past lessons.
- An ideal schedule would be at least five times a week for about 20 minutes per session.

Why does this seem so repetitive?

Children love repetition, and it drives learning. If you use this book and think, "That's repetitive, isn't this the same as the last game?" just know it's been designed that way.

How can I give my child a hint?

Trace the letter on the child's back or in the air to give the child a hint, e.g., "Can you find 'ah'? It looks like this (trace letter in the air)."

What if my child keeps getting it wrong?

- After a few tries, say, "Here it is! Next time you'll learn it. We're only practicing."
- Keep it light and fun.
- Remember, children often forget how to do something new, and with time, repetition, and practice, your child will master reading the words with ease.

What should I do if my child is having trouble focusing?

- EAT/REST — Make sure your child has eaten and is well rested before starting a lesson.
- ENCOURAGEMENT — Recognize how hard your child is working and encourage them, e.g., "I know you can do this, and I'm here to do it with you."
- FOLLOW THE CHILD — If you feel that your child is not engaging with the book, stop for a little while and reintroduce it at another time.
- REMIND THEM OF IMPORTANCE — This is critical: you need to inform your child that reading is a wonderful and powerful thing, e.g., "You can pick up a book and enjoy a story. Reading is a power that adults have...let's learn it together!"

What if my child only knows "B" and finds it confusing to say "buh"?

Explain to your child, "I'm glad that you know your capitals, but we can't read by saying 'ABC.' We read by saying 'ah,' 'buh,' 'ck,' which are the letter sounds."

Why are we only learning lowercase letters?

- Only five percent of written material is made of uppercase letters. By teaching the lowercase letters first, children learn 26 sounds instead of 52 symbols.
- Do not worry — children learn uppercase letters easily as they become readers.

FAQ

Do I have to read the whole book?

- No. You can stop at the end of any lesson and restart at any time.
- You can also restart at any point in the book, depending on how well your child has grasped each lesson.

Is it okay to skip a section?

Yes. If your child has mastered a section, focus on the other sections that are still challenging.

How can we integrate lessons into life?

- GAMES — Play "I Spy" with your child, e.g., "I spy with my little eye, something that starts with 'buh.' Can you tell me what object it is?"
- ART — Make letters into fun art projects, e.g., "Let's make the letter 'ah' and put pictures on it of things that start with 'ah.'"
- ACTIVITIES — Put cornmeal/salt/sand in a shallow pan and trace letters. Then shake to reset.
- MATCH — Ask your child to fetch objects starting with a certain letter.
- LETTER BOOKS — Children love making personal books. Write (or have your child write) letters and words they are learning in a notebook.

When is my child ready for the next book?

Lesson 3 (Guess the Letter) is a good way to make sure children can recall letters. If they can play this game with ease, they are ready for the Orange Books.

What if my child is still having trouble after one month (and is already four to six-years-old)?

- Every child's pace is different.
- Don't give up — find ways to keep it fun and exciting and to integrate lessons into your child's daily life.
- Some children have a learning difference (such as dyslexia). If you suspect your child has a learning difference, have them tested (often done in kindergarten).
- In the meantime, this book is your tool to support your child — it is particularly effective at helping dyslexic children learn to read.
- Remind your child that every brain is different and that they will learn too!

Made in the USA
Columbia, SC
10 September 2019